DEVOTIONS FOR DIETERS

INSPIRED LIVING SERIES
DEVOTIONS FOR DIETERS

BY

CECIL MURPHEY
New York Times Bestselling Author

eISBN: 978-1-937776-17-6
ISBN 13: 978-1-937776-89-3

OTHER BOOKS BY CECIL MURPHEY

Inspired Living Devotional Series:

Devotions for Couples
Devotions for Dieters
Devotions for Runners
Revitalize Your Prayer Life: Inspired
Living Series Companion

More Titles:

90 Minutes in Heaven (with Don Piper)
Gifted Hands: The Ben Carson
Story (with Dr. Ben Carson)
Rebel with a Cause (with Franklin Graham)
Because You Care: Spiritual Encouragement for
Caregivers (by Cecil Murphey and Twila Belk)
When Someone You Love No Longer Remembers
The Spirit of Christmas (by Cecil
Murphey and Marley Gibson)
Unleash the Writer Within
Knowing God, Knowing Myself
When a Man You Love Was Abused
When God Turned Off the Lights

A New Beginning

I wrote this book nearly 30 years ago, shortly after I first learned about nutrition and health. I saw excellent results and, like most new converts, I was zealous to change the world.

In this book, you'll realize I was never obese and my personal weight problems may seem far smaller than yours. But obese, overweight, chubby, or pleasantly plump all come down to one thing: We need to make changes. It's as much our self-perception as it is the way others see us.

And one major change is to lose weight and keep it off. New information comes at us with medical and scientific breakthroughs.

The information in the book is still solid. I advocated running—and still do—but I've also realized that most people do better with walking. And that means brisk, fast-paced, and energetic. Some do the power-walking thing with exaggerated movements and a dumbbell in either hand.

I haven't counted calories for 20 years, but I'm careful about the way I eat.

But one thing hasn't changed: Most people still struggle with their weight. According to the statistics from the Center for Disease Control and Prevention, about two-thirds of Americans are overweight. If there is any question in our minds, go into any public area and look at the people who pass by.

I decided fairly early that weight loss wasn't my goal. My goal was a healthy lifestyle. At the time of this writing, I am 78 years old, and I stay within two pounds of my target weight.

When I began to change my lifestyle, my blood pressure was at the high-normal range and my doctor told me that I'd soon on blood-pressure medicine.

I've never needed that medication. In fact, at age 78, I take no meds, eat three healthy meals each day, get plenty of sleep. I'm still highly productive and write at least two books a year.

In all of this, I'm thankful to God for teaching me and guiding me to observe one powerful-but-often-neglected command. The Apostle Paul wrote, "I plead with you to give your bodies to God because of all he has done for you. Let them be a living and holy sacrifice—the kind he will find acceptable" (Romans 12:1a).

STARTING RIGHT

Satisfy us each morning with your unfailing love, so we may sing for joy to the end of our lives. (Psalm 90:14)

Week 1, Day 1

"I never eat breakfast," Alice said, as though that proved a badge of commendation. She prided herself on avoiding breakfast and eating nothing until lunch. She advised the rest of us to cut down to two meals a day or, even better, just one. I might have listened more seriously, but Alice weighs nearly 300 pounds.

Her theory sounded all right: don't get the appetite going in the morning and you will keep it under control all day. It sounds good, but it doesn't work.

First, people who skip breakfast are unusually hungry by noon and ready to eat all day. In a survey on the eating habits of teens, conducted a few years ago by a University of California professor, the obese tended to skip breakfast.

Second, we need the energy for the peak of the day. Even if your breakfast consists of only 200 or 300 calories, you need both protein and complex carbohydrates. If we eliminate the first meal of the day, we lose out on stepped-up metabolism by many hours and tend to overeat at dinner. We require more calories in the active part of the day when we need energy and our system is working at its best. If we do most of our eating in the evening, we tend to store up fat.

Good nutrition starts with that first meal of the day, just as good spiritual life begins in the morning.

We're at our best for the Lord when we start our morning with time devoted to praying and Bible study, our spiritual food and defense against the enemies of our soul that we'll encounter during the day.

The most important part of my day begins with the morning: a good breakfast, and a special time with Jesus Christ.

Lord Jesus, like the psalmist, help me seek you early so that I can feed my soul. Teach me, too, to enjoy a nutritious breakfast to fill my body. Amen.

OR WHATEVER

So whether you eat or drink, or whatever you do, do it all for the glory of God. (1 Corinthians 10:31)

Week 1, Day 2

For about four years I had realized my need to think seriously about weight control. Occasionally I would cut back at a meal, or even refuse a dessert. But I never seriously did anything about it. Two things helped make me a calorie counter. One was a result of a physical from my doctor, in which he warned me that my blood pressure was beginning to elevate.

The second thing was this verse, 1 Corinthians 10:31. I tried to push it out of my mind on several occasions, but it really stuck with me. Then one day I made a commitment. I decided that my body would no longer be the garbage heap, that I would lose weight, that I would treat my body the way God wanted it to be treated.

This verse has also reminded me that what I eat and drink are only symbols of the rest of my life. The real crux of it comes out in the latter part of that verse, "So whether you eat or drink, or whatever you do, do it all for the glory of God." The biggest implication for me of 1 Corinthians 10:31 is that it pushes me to make Jesus Christ the Lord of my entire life.

Lord Jesus, I say the word Lord *so easily. Help me mean it in every thought, in every word, in every deed. Amen.*

THE HOLY BODY

Don't you realize that all of you together are the temple of God and that the Spirit of God lives in you? (1 Corinthians 3:16)

Week 1, Day 3

It came as a shock to me to realize that the Apostle Paul calls the body the temple of the Holy Spirit. His recorders of the first century would have understood that much more clearly than we. They thought of the tabernacle or the temple as that special place where God dwelt. They kept it clean; they followed minute instructions in its maintenance. Certainly, then, Paul is saying that we're to give care to our body.

This is not only to please God. It's also for our own benefit. Obesity is a definite health hazard. Somehow we tend to think of obese people as jolly, always full of life. Often that's only a cover-up. Obesity walks hand in hand with chronic diseases and early death. The burden of extra weight we haul around every minute takes its toll. Countless studies have proven that fat people are more likely to develop degenerative diseases and to die at younger ages than those of normal weight. Overweight people are more prone to cancer, diabetes, strokes, heart attacks, high blood pressure, and kidney diseases.

The knowledge that my body is God's holy temple and his dwelling-place encourages me to keep the rules—that is, to watch the way I eat, to be a slimmer me. The more seriously I believe in Jesus Christ and observe his commandments, the more faithfully I watch what I eat and count the calories.

Holy Spirit, remind me that my body is yours. Help me to take care of it faithfully. Amen.

EXCUSES, EXCUSES, EXCUSES

But they all began making excuses. One said, 'I have just bought a field and must inspect it. Please excuse me.' (Luke 14:18)

Week 1, Day 4

Calorie counters have something in common with alcoholics and compulsive gamblers. Most heavy people, like alcoholics, don't get significant changes or achieve lasting results until they stop making excuses. There are plenty of excuses people use. Here are the three I hear most often.

"I never eat anything fattening." A corpulent friend used to say that very regularly. One time she invited us to her home for a meal. She must have eaten two ounces of gravy, at least an ounce of mashed potatoes, and small portions of four or five other foods while she was cooking. When she actually put the food on the table, she did not use the gravy and she avoided salad dressing, but earlier...

"I never eat much." The folks who say that are usually the nibblers. They nibble at cookies. They sip a bottle of pop. What they don't realize is that each of

those calories counts. When you stop to think about it, two potato chips or a saltine cracker really don't add up to very much. But when you add potato chips, a cracker, four cookies, two bottles of pop, a tiny piece of pizza, and a small helping of ice cream, all as snacks before lunch, it adds up.

"My problem is glandular." Of course it's glandular; we make it that way. Anybody seriously overweight has a system that is not efficient and no longer functions properly. The thyroid becomes sluggish, the hypothalamus and pituitary glands go out of whack. Why not? They don't know how to cope with the large abundance of food that is put into the body.

"I'm too busy to exercise." "I was a fat baby." "People my age put on weight." The excuses go on and on. We have to realize that they are only excuses.

If we're going to lose weight, we start by being honest with ourselves. We acknowledge our extra poundage and determine to do something about it. And finally, we stop making excuses. When we honestly admit that we simply *eat too much,* we can then call upon Jesus Christ to help us with our problem.

Loving Father, forgive me for making excuses. Help me to be honest with myself and to be faithful in counting every calorie. Amen.

THE BEST DIET

For instance, one person believes it's all right to eat any-thing. But another believer with a sensitive conscience will eat only vegetables. Those who feel free to eat anything must not look down on those who don't. And those who don't eat certain foods must not condemn those who do, for God has accepted them. (Romans 14:2–3)

Week 1, Day 5

Which is the best diet? Answer: The one that works for you. We have different metabolisms and different taste patterns. Nancy dropped Weight Watchers because she simply could not get used to eating fish. A friend of mine tried popular low-carb diet and although she lost weight, she felt listless all the time. Polly tried a high protein, low carbohy-drate diet and, at twenty-one, ended up with gout.

There is no right diet that fits everyone. There are also no shortcuts. Those who took appetite depressants, so bountiful a generation ago, learned that. If they took the pills too long, they became addicted to them. If they left the medication, they ballooned again.

The right diet for any of us involves discipline and commitment. If it's the right diet, it also involves common sense. It contains a balance, so that we lack nothing in nutrition. Popping vitamins to compensate for fad diets isn't the answer either. While vitamins aid, they are not intended as substitutes for proper nutrition.

The matter of dieting and eating has always been a problem in the world. The Apostle Paul dealt with it when he wrote to the Romans. He says some eat only vegetables because they are weak, while others eat anything. He adds that what a person eats makes no real difference. "…Those who eat any kind of food do so to honor the Lord, since they give thanks to God before eating. And those who refuse to eat certain foods also want to please the Lord and give thanks to God" (Romans 14:6).

What diet is best for me? Not the one that merely helps me get results, but the one that also helps keep the weight off. It takes commitment and discipline for that.

Lord Jesus, help me find the right diet for me, and then help me discipline myself and strengthen my commitment. Amen.

How Much Can I Eat?

If you are a big eater, put a knife to your throat.
(Proverbs 23:2)

Week 1, Day 6

How do I get rid of extra pounds? Simple—at least mathematically. I must take in sufficiently lower calories to cause body fat to be burned (or oxidized) for fuel. Since one pound of body fat represents about 3,500 calories of stored energy, for each 3,500 calories of energy used by my body *beyond* that provided by the food I eat, I can expect to shed a pound.

On the other hand, for every 3,500 calories more that I eat which my body does not need, I gain a pound. Simple math.

How do you find an acceptable level of calorie intake? I determine my desired weight by consulting tables prepared by the United States Department of Agriculture, Metropolitan Insurance Company, or other charts. Then I multiply my desired pounds by fifteen calories per pound to find the approximate number of calories I can use from my food supply to maintain this weight.

If, for instance, I need 2,250 calories a day for my size (I think of myself here as 150 pounds), then I must eat less than 2,250 calories each day to lose weight. As soon as I chalk up 3,500 calories *not* eaten, I can expect to lose a pound.

It all comes down to one thing: I have to reduce the amount of the food I eat to lose pounds. We've overeaten for a long time. Now we want to train ourselves to eat less. As we learn the caloric value of what we eat and count up every calorie we put in our mouths, we become winners in the losing game.

Heavenly Father, teach me to restrain my eating so that I can truly lose weight. Amen.

UNHELPFUL FRIENDS

Even my best friend, the one I trusted completely, the one who shared my food, had turned against me. (Psalm 41:9)

Week 1, Day 7

When I started counting calories, the first thing I did was to eliminate rich desserts from my diet. I did not need them and decided that for the rest of my life they would not be in my diet. The biggest problem didn't involve my commitment, but my friends.

At a church supper, I was going through the line, carefully passing up desserts, which included pecan pie and strawberry shortcake. Someone behind me said, "Why aren't you eating any dessert?"

I said something to the effect that I was not having any because I was dieting.

My friend looked at me, frowned, and said, "You intimidate people like me. You make us feel guilty because you pass those desserts by." He took a second look at me and said, "You don't really need to lose any weight. You're thin enough now." I looked at my friend who was at least a hundred pounds overweight and assumed that by his standards I was skinny. By my standards, I still had ten pounds to lose.

Often when we're counting calories and trying to lose weight, our friends make it difficult for us. One thing I finally said to a few friends who kept after me was, "Help me lose weight. Help me be more pleased with the way I look and the way I see myself." The real friends understood.

Lord Jesus, some of your friends turned out to be enemies, often without realizing it. Help me to lose weight, and help my friends encourage me. Amen.

GETTING THERE

For all who are led by the Spirit of God are children of God.
(Romans 8:14)

Week 2, Day 1

When I decided to lose weight, I read a number of books about dieting. Every book had a different plan and for a while it confused me. Then I discovered basic facts. First, all the diets work. If you follow any diet faithfully, you lose weight. That includes the Spinach Diet, the Egg Diet, the Watercress Diet, the Grapefruit Diet, and some of the more popularly named ones—they all work.

But the problem is most of them don't work for long. Most of the diets are faddish or crash diets. They work on the principle of teaching people to do without certain foods for a period of tie. Then when they get down to an ideal weight, they can begin adding those foods back into their diet. I saw the mistake of that right away.

I decided that when I lost weight, I was going to learn to eat sensibly and plan to eat that way for the rest of my life. Any changes I made in my diet or in my life-style would be permanent.

The significant decision to count calories hinges on a commitment and a strong desire. It means changing your style of life.

That's the same requirement involved in following Jesus Christ as a disciple. Paul says in Romans 8:14 that as many as are led by the Spirit of God are sons of God. He points out that we mature by obeying God and listening to his Spirit and allowing the Spirit to lead us.

It works the same way whether we're talking about counting calories, an exercise program, or devotional studies. We need to make a commitment. We need to ask Jesus Christ to help us and then allow the Holy Spirit to lead us. With the Spirit's help we can maintain the commitment we make and eventually achieve the goals we set for ourselves.

Holy Spirit, teach me to be led by you in the way I eat, in the way I live, in every part of my life. Amen.

IGNORANCE PAYS

Regarding your question about the special abilities the Spirit gives us. I don't want you to misunderstand this. (1 Corinthians 12:1)

Week 2, Day 2

In my mid-thirties I became aware of my increased weight. "I'll have to do something about it," I said to myself and my wife several times.

Then I took the plunge and started out. Over the years I had accumulated incorrect information such as: proteins help you lose weight and carbohydrates make you gain. For the next week I loaded up on protein—eating meat almost exclusively, and lots of it. I particularly liked salami, polish sausage, and pork chops. Somehow that idea didn't work. I actually put on two pounds.

I tried cutting out desserts and eliminating sugar and milk in my coffee. However, a little marmalade on my toast didn't count much. Ice milk wasn't as fattening as ice cream. I kept gaining.

It took a few more years and frustrated dieting before I realized a stark truth: ignorance pays the wrong kind of dividends.

Like a lot of people who wanted to drop off the pounds, I went about it the wrong way. It was only when I learned about nutrition and sensible calorie counting that the excess baggage started disappearing.

The Apostle Paul understood about ignorance. He wrote to the Corinthian church about that very subject. They had been a greatly blessed church—he said in the first chapter that they lacked nothing in spiritual gifts. But the apostle had a lot of straightening out to do with that local congregation. In chapters 12–14 he wrote about the meaning, purpose, and use of these gifts. But he prefaced his remarks with these words: "Now concerning spiritual gifts, brethren, I do not want you to be uninformed."

Because they had been ignorant, they had all kinds of confusion in that congregation. He wrote to enlighten them and set them straight.

Knowing we need to lose weight, plus a few isolated facts, aren't enough. We need to learn about nutrition. We need to learn how our body operates. As we learn more, we not only rid ourselves of misinformation, but we learn how to slim down and live with a body that's healthier and happier.

Great Teacher, help me learn about calories and losing weight. Don't let me foolishly do all the wrong things in a misguided attempt to drop off pounds. Amen.

IDEAL WEIGHTS

Peter asked Jesus, "What about him, Lord?" (John 21:21)

Week 2, Day 3

What's the ideal weight? Insurance companies publish a list of average weights for men and women. One of the running books I read suggest that runners figure their ideal weight by taking their height in inches and doubling that amount. If I am six feet tall, that means 144 pounds. That's too thin for most of us.

I've seen other charts which figure 100 pounds for five feet tall and five pounds for each additional inch. For the six-footer, that works out to a weight of 160. That's not bad.

The truth is, there's no such thing as an *ideal* weight that applies to everyone. We're all individuals and there's no yardstick that applies to every single person.

When I went on my serious and permanent weight loss program I aimed at 140. That's approximately the weight I had when I was twenty-two. I chose that size because I "felt" comfortable at that figure.

For me, and for all of us, we have that weight where we feel right about ourselves.

As I think of this, it reminds me of an incident in Peter's life. After the resurrection, Jesus told the number one apostle that "when you are old, you will stretch out your hands, and others will dress you and take you where you don't want to go" (John 21:18). By this he foretold Peter's death.

Later, Peter saw John and asked, "What about him, Lord?" Jesus replied, "If I want him to remain alive until I return, what is that to you? As for you, follow me." (John 21:22)

Peter had one mission—watch out for Peter. John had his own destiny to worry about. That applies to weight loss, service to Jesus Christ, or living in general. Christ holds me responsible for *me*.

Jesus, help me find my ideal weight, just as I have found my ideal in your example and in your death for me. Amen.

PASS THE SUGAR—PLEASE

It is not good to eat much honey. (Proverbs 25:27)

Week 2, Day 4

Know why the Bible doesn't speak about sugar? It was hardly known in those days. They had honey—quite a lot of it—and the wise man of Proverbs advised against much honey because he knew the danger of too much sweetness.

Refined sugar, that lovely white stuff, is not a natural food, but a chemical with no food value! Chemically it's known as $Cl_{12}H_{22}O_{11}$. Yet this non-food finds its way into just about everything we buy: peanut butter, catsup, canned soup, luncheon meats, peas, bread, and salad dressings. It's the number two ingredient in many products. *It's also addictive.*

The average person in the United States eats almost 100 pounds of the white granules every year, and this amount could add forty-five pounds a year to a heavy sugar consumer. Experts estimate that 20 percent of our diet consists of sugar. That's all sugar is, something that makes us fat—without vitamins, minerals, protein, or fiber. It is just empty calories. And it's as addictive as nicotine or alcohol.

To paint the picture darker, experts such as Doctors John Yudkin and David Reuben (along with hosts of others) blame excessive sugar consumption for the rise in atherosclerosis (coating of the arteries with fatty substances), which leads to heart attacks. They also list it as a leading cause of diabetes, indigestion, skin disease, gout, myopia, and tooth decay.

Shirley and I have become avid label readers. We do this, not only out of concern for our weight, but because we both believe in the sanctity of the body. My body is God's holy dwelling-place, and he gives *me* responsibility and holds *me* accountable for the way I take care of it. I want it to be a healthy temple for the Spirit.

Lord of power, give me strength to eliminate anything from my diet which does not make me stronger and healthier. Especially help me kick the sugar habit. Amen.

ADD THE BRAN

"At the end of the ten days, see how we look compared to the other young men who are eating the king's food. Then make your decision in light of what you see." The attendant agreed to Daniel's suggestion and tested them for ten days.

At the end of the ten days, Daniel and his three friends looked healthier and better nourished than the young men who had been eating the food assigned by the king. So after that, the attendant fed them only vegetables instead of the food and wine provided for the others. (Daniel 1:13-16)

Week 2, Day 5

While visiting with missionary friends in rural Costa Rica, we stopped at a café. By the side of the road, I saw strange piles of what appeared to be wood shavings. "What's that?" I asked.

"The residue from the rice," my friend said. "After milling the rice so that it's white, they throw the rest of it away."

I shook my head. Rice, along with beans, provides the staple food item for the people. Yet they throw away the most nutritious part.

This happens not only in Costa Rica, but all over the Western world. Since the late 1800s it has become fashionable to get rid of roughage in grains.

More and more experts are urging us to add bran as a dietary fiber to our meals. Bran is fairly cheap, and we can add up to three tablespoons daily to cereals, cottage cheese, soups, meat loaf, or other ground meats. We've discovered that adding dietary fiber such as bran actually increases weight loss.

It works like this. A high-roughage diet requires more time to eat because we have to chew more thoroughly. High fiber eating leads our stomachs to feel full long before we overeat. We actually end up eating less. As we chew high-fiber foods. They mix with large amounts of saliva and gastric juices, which causes the fibers in the food to swell, giving a sense of being full.

It appears that in his time Daniel figured out the significance of proper nutrition, even without our modern research. By adhering to the strict dietary laws of Moses, Daniel knew he would be healthy and strong.

Daniel, carried captive from Israel by the Babylonians, moved into the king's palace. He, along with other bright young men, were trained for leadership. Daniel, however, refused to eat the "king's rich food" (Daniel 1:8) and insisted on veg-etables and water. After a ten-day trial, Daniel and his friends were healthier than the others.

Daniel knew what to eat, stood his ground, and followed the knowledge he had. In turn, God made him healthier than those who ate the rich foods of the king.

God, as I learn more about nutrition, help me put my knowledge into practice so I will become healthier and thinner. Amen.

GOAL-SETTING

I focus on this one thing: Forgetting the past and looking forward to what lies ahead. (Philippians 3:13)

Week 2, Day 6

Life is filled with goals. We have to meet certain standards in order to get a driver's license. We have to set goals and meet them in order to graduate from high school or college. Even when we want to purchase something, we have to meet the goal—that is, have enough money to pay for the item. Goal-setting is part of our way of life.

The Apostle Paul knew about this. In the third chapter of Philippians he gives an autobiographical account of his background. He tells of all the advantages he had in being born a Jew and being of the tribe of Benjamin. He was a man of education and knowledge. But Paul went on to say that's really nothing; the real goal is Jesus Christ. "Forgetting the past and looking forward to what lies ahead, I press on to reach the end of the race and receive the heavenly prize for which God, through Christ Jesus is calling us" (Philippians 3:13–14). He had his goal and would settle for nothing less.

You're a calorie counter. What kind of goal have you set for yourself? Don't make your goal a general one to lose weight. How many pounds do you wish to lose? Ten? Fifty? Ninety-three? Probably the greatest reward of goal-setting is goal-reaching.

I remember when I had lost twenty-five pounds; I was very happy. A week later I still had kept off the twenty-five pounds, and now five years later I've actually lost an additional five. I felt pleased with myself. I'd set a goal, I made it. There's something about setting goals and reaching them that gives me a good feeling inside.

I failed a few times along the way, and there were a few weeks when I actually gained weight. There were a few times when I overindulged or under exercised, or both. I accepted those times as temporary setbacks and still aimed for my goal. You can do the same.

Heavenly Father, help me not only to set my goal as a calorie counter but to stick with it until I obtain it. Amen.

OVERSETTING GOALS

This is the day the LORD has made. We will rejoice and be glad in it. (Psalm 118:24)

Week 2, Day 7

One lesson I learned about weight control came through working with Alcoholics Anonymous. They have a lot of catchy phrases to encourage each other. One of them is: *One day at a time.*

They don't try to stay sober for a year. Not even six months. They aim for one day. Each day an alcoholic asks for strength for *this* day.

Jesus taught this principle. He said, "Do not be anxious about tomorrow, for tomorrow will be anxious for itself. Let the day's own trouble be sufficient for the day."

The AAs also have another saying, "Easy does it." It's a reminder to them to take everything as it comes. Handle one problem at a time. Fight each temptation as it hits and don't concentrate on the battles still ahead.

The more we concentrate on the amount we still have to lose, the more depressing it becomes, and the bigger that amount appears.

One friend said, "When I lost weight, I kept thinking to myself, I'm a better me today. I'm thinner today than I was yesterday, and I have more self-confidence and self-control."

That's the way to approach it. We have a goal down the line we work toward, but we concentrate on counting our calories today. Don't get concerned about failing next weekend or when vacation time rolls around. Concentrate on today, and ask Jesus Christ for strength to make it through. The Apostle Paul said it this way: "For I can do everything through Christ, who gives me strength" (Philippians 4:13).

Loving God, remind me that today is my immediate concern. Help me control my appetite today. Amen.

FACING MYSELF

But don't just listen to God's word. You must do what it says. Otherwise, you are only fooling yourselves. For if you listen to the word and don't obey, it is like glancing at your face in a mirror. You see yourself, walk away, and forget what you look like. (James 1:22–24)

Week 3, Day 1

I'll never forget the day that I made my decision to count calories. I had come out of the shower, and standing in the bathroom I saw a side view of myself. I didn't like what I saw: a paunchy stomach, flabby arms, thickening thighs, a collar size a full inch bigger than it had ever been before in my life. That's when I decided to do something about it. And I did! I determined that day I would begin to count calories and would not stop until I had lost at least twenty-five pounds.

That may not sound like a lot of weight for some people to lose, but every pound is hard to lose. It meant not only a commitment to counting calories, a strict discipline, but it also entailed at least two other things.

First, I had to be *honest* with God and myself. I wanted to lose weight. I determined to become a trim person, even when old habits kept attacking me. I often prayed, "Lord, help me stick to my diet, even when I don't want to."

The other thing is, I knew I would fail once in a while. I had to learn to forgive myself. Forgiving myself meant saying to God and to Cec, "Okay, you blew it. Do better next time."

I learned that I couldn't just see that I needed to lose weight, I had to do something about it. By acting on my concern, I became the kind of person the Apostle James commends when he says it isn't enough to hear God's Word. We must also obey it. Those who only hear are like people who see themselves in a mirror and then forget what they look like. I had seen my flabby self many times and quickly erased the visual image. But the day I started to count calories I not only saw my image; I determined to change it. With God's help I have done that.

Lord Jesus, thank you for showing me myself. Help me to remember what I look like and give me a vision of what I can be. Amen.

SHOW AND TELL

I discipline my body like an athlete, training it to do what it should. Otherwise, I fear that after preaching to others I myself might be disqualified. (1 Corinthians 9:27)

Week 3, Day 2

One day I walked into the steam room at the health spa. A man sat in the middle of the room explaining to three others about vitamins, minerals, and proper nutrition. He delivered a lecture on complementary proteins and balanced meals and the importance of nutrition and vitamin supplements.

I would have been greatly impressed by everything he said, except for one thing. I stared at a man at least seventy-five pounds overweight. He may have had all the facts about nutrition, but he certainly did not apply them to himself. It became evident that he was not in good physical shape himself, even aside from being overweight, because eventually he mentioned his high blood pressure and his heart condition.

I constantly meet people like the man at the spa. They know al the right answers. They can tell you everything there is to know about dieting; they can tell you almost anything you want to know about any subject. The trouble is, they don't live by their own words.

My father did not know Jesus Christ until he was eighty-four, a short time before he died. But my dad knew a lot about the Bible and frequently quoted Bible verses. He knew the way, but didn't choose to walk in it.

We all need to look at ourselves once in a while to ask if we're living by what we're professing. The Apostle Paul said that he disciplined his body so that when the time of real judgment came, he would not be rejected as one who professed but did not possess. The Living Bible translates the verse this way: "Like an athlete I punish my body, treating it roughly, training it to do what it should, not what it wants to. Otherwise I fear that after enlisting others for the race, I myself might be declared unfit and ordered to stand aside."

Perhaps the best way to teach others about calorie counting, or anything else in life, is by example. Another way to say it is: *show* me, then you can *tell* me.

Holy God, help me to learn about counting calories. But even more, enable me to put that information into practice in my own life. Amen.

ONLY A LITTLE FAILURE

See, there is a small village nearby. Please let me go there instead; don't you see how small it is? Then my life will be saved." (Genesis 19:20)

Week 3, Day 3

When I first started to lose weight, a lovely shut-in from our congregation liked doing kind things for me. She lived alone and had few visitors. I made it a point to drop in on her twice a month. She wanted to repay my kindness in a tangible way, and so she began to make me cherry cheesecakes.

Every time I visited, she would have a cherry cheesecake ready for me. The first time I brought it home, set it on the kitchen table, and said, "It looks so good, I'll eat just a tiny sliver." It was not on my diet, but it was a small piece.

No one else was home and in a few minutes I thought, *Another tiny sliver won't hurt much,* and I cut another piece, quite small. Fifteen minutes later I did it again. After gobbling it down, I looked at the cherry cheesecake and realized that I had by now cut a fairly good-sized piece. I thought, *Oh, well, I've blown it now,* so I took another piece.

My wife arrived home two hours later. I had eaten half of that cherry cheesecake. That half cherry cheesecake set me back on my diet and taught me that to give in the first time opens the door for other lapses.

I had underestimated the importance of little failures. Had someone suggested I eat half a cheesecake, I would have refused and probably said, "What are you trying to do to me?"

A little piece seemed so small. But it's the little failures that cause us the most trouble.

The little failures count up, just like calories.

Mighty God, remind me of the little lapses. Give me strength to hold out against them. Amen.

Secret Sins

You spread out our sins before you—our secret sins—and you see them all. (Psalm 90:8)

Week 3, Day 4

A health spa sign proclaimed, WHAT YOU EAT IN PRIVATE SHOWS UP IN PUBLIC. Next to the sign stood the scales. For me this graphically illustrates that we get away with nothing. Some people on diets seem to think that a tiny cookie, an extra spoonful of mashed potatoes and gravy, or only a small piece of cake won't count; no one will know. But we never really get away with anything. Still we keep trying to deceive others and ourselves.

Sometimes I've watched people eat forbidden food or extra amounts, discount it with a smile and say, "I'll have to run around the block a couple of extra times." I don't think they ever run around the block a couple of extra times. Even if they did, that wouldn't make up for the overindulgence.

We all get caught in the secret sin syndrome. Sometimes we think we can do something wrong— a sin which isn't very bad—and it won't count. Or later we can ask God to forgive us and no one will know. But no sin is ever secret, because God knows.

We need to remind ourselves that when we count calories we're not only helping our bodies; we're also trying to please God, and we don't please him by cheating.

Lord God, as a calorie counter help me to be honest with you and with myself, in public or in secret. Amen.

ANYTHING FOR A
PIECE OF PIE

Esau said to Jacob, "I'm starved! Give me some of that red stew!" (This is how Esau got his other name, Edom, which means "red.") "All right," Jacob replied, "but trade me your rights as the firstborn son." "Look, I'm dying of starvation!" said Esau. "What good is my birthright to me now?" (Genesis 25:30-32)

Week 3, Day 5

In those early days of calorie counting, we crave foods—usually those high in sugar or fat (or both). I've heard dieters talk of how they miss their pecan pie and have seen them drool as they nibbled on lettuce or bit a celery stalk. Sometimes the temptation becomes too great, and they sell their diets for a slice of pecan pie.

In the Bible a man sold his life for less than that. Esau, the firstborn son of Isaac, had been out hunting for a long time. On his return he met his brother Jacob, who had boiled a pot of vegetables. Esau was so hungry, he traded his birthright for a bowl of vegetable soup.

Saint Paul, in writing to Titus, referred to the people of Crete (quoting one of their own poets) as "lazy gluttons" (Titus 1:12 V), implying that they cared more for the contents of their stomachs than anything else.

Some of us have realized our bellies often rule us. We're constantly thinking about food—the meal we're eating or the one we want to eat next. If only we could find a magic elixir that would enable us to eat anything we want and gain no pounds, we'd almost sell our soul for the formula.

Does it sound extreme to say that? I know that when I started calorie counting, I was not only hungry most of the time, but I thought far more about food than ever before. I thought of the privations and the things I was resisting. When I'd go into restaurants, I'd have to force myself not to look at the luscious meals others ate. I learned, in time, to like my salad bar, but it didn't come easy.

Not only did I overcome the temptations of giving in to my desires, but it also taught me who my true God was. Paul spoke of some by saying, "their god is their appetite" (Philippians 3:19).

My dieting began with a concern for my physical condition, after my doctor warned me of my creeping high blood pressure and my children kidded me about wearing a football inside my stomach. But the real clincher for me was spiritual. I wanted to please Christ and give him control over my life.

Holy Lord, I want you to rule my life. Help in my calorie counting, so that you and I both know that you're the real Lord of my life. Amen.

BEATING THE MUNCHIES

… Fix your thoughts on what is true, and honorable, and right, and pure, and lovely, and admirable. Think about things that are excellent and worthy of praise. (Philippians 4:8)

Week 3, Day 6

Shirley went back to college a couple of years ago. She's bright, and even graduated from high school twentieth in a class of several hundred. She studies hard all through every course, beginning with the first day. But I can always tell when she faces a midterm or final exam.

I can tell by watching her snacking behavior. She always nibbles when studying, but it intensifies during exam periods. While she always does exceptionally well on tests, I suspect that inside she fears she'll fail or do less than her best.

She calls this her "munchies." Another way of talking about it is to call it *anxiety,* even worry. The Apostle Paul wrote to the Philippians that they shouldn't be anxious about anything. Instead, he exhorted them to pray, give thanks, and tell God all about it. Paul then assures them they'll receive God's peace. That's the best way to beat anxiety: pray until we have the Lord's peace in our hearts.

All kinds of things stir up our anxiety, and none of us ever grow completely free. We learn to cope. We discover what works for us. I've talked to a few formerly fat folks and here are ideas that they developed.

Allow yourself one cracker and see how long you can make it last.

Try chewing sugarless gum. It keeps your mouth busy, and yet allows no real food or calories inside.

How about physical exercise (a few calisthenics or even a walk around the block)? The physical activity uses up the nervous energy.

You may have another idea that works for you. The main thing is, don't give in to the munchies. Those little munchie times put on pounds. And because you're determined to be thin, you can beat the munchies.

Lord Jesus, I want to lose weight. When I go through periods of anxiety, help me find my peace in you, not through food. Amen.

Giving Up

But the one who endures to the end will be saved.
(Matthew 24:13)

Week 3, Day 7

I was talking to Travis the other day. He's one of those people who's on a perpetual diet. He said to me, "Well, this diet I'm on now isn't going to work."

"Why not?" I asked.

"Well," he said, "I've been on it seven days and I've only lost three pounds."

I didn't try to argue with Travis. I didn't try to say to him, "Two or three pounds a week is considered a safe and a fairly good amount of weight to lose." I didn't say those things because I've known Travis for a long time. He's tried all the diets. Dr. Stillman's diet, Dr. Atkins', Weight Watchers, the Cellulite Diet, the Boston Police Diet, the Pritkin Diet, and probably dozens of others that I've never heard of. The trouble is, Travis never stays on any of them very long; he gives up too soon.

Some people seem to be that way. They start projects but never finish, have great ideas but never bring them to completion. The way people approach the gospel is like that, too. Some start well, but give up midway. Or they start with a lot of zeal and wear out when things get tough.

Jesus said to his disciples, "He who endures to the end will be saved." He talked about persevering through tribulations and ultimate salvation.

The same exhortation applies to calorie counters. Don't give up. You've made a commitment to become a slimmer, better you. You can make it! And remember, God wants you to succeed.

Holy Savior, enable me to stick with my diet. Help me daily to realize how much you love me and that you're ready to help me when I need you. Amen.

UGLY DUCKLINGS

"Don't be afraid!" David said. "I intend to show kindness to you because of my promise to your father, Jonathan. I will give you all the property that once belonged to your grandfather Saul, and you will eat here with me at the king's table!" (2 Samuel 9:7)

Week 4, Day 1

Eve, at least one hundred pounds overweight, sat in my office telling me about one problem after another in her home. She finally said, "Sometimes I can hardly stand myself. I just want to go away and die."

Eve and I talked some more and when I asked about her weight, she told me that she hates mirrors. Every time she looks in a mirror, it reminds her how ugly she is. She didn't say *fat,* she said *ugly.* Like other fat people, she thinks of herself as ugly because in her mind, ugly and fat are synonymous words.

We need to remind ourselves that we may be too heavy, but that does not mean we are ugly. We may be eighty pounds overweight, but God still declares us beautiful.

A story in the Old Testament illustrates God's view of beauty. David had become the king of Israel. He wanted to show kindness to the family of his friend Jonathan, who had died in battle. David heard about Mephibosheth, who was lame.

In those days, lameness meant lack of being whole. Physically handicapped people could not come into the king's presence. David called Mephibosheth in anyway and he said, "As long as you live, you may sit at my table and eat of my food." He even promised to restore to Mephibosheth the land that had been lost.

What did Mephibosheth do? He bowed down, said he was like a dead dog, and asked why David should show honor to him.

What we often fail to realize is that grace works that way. God loves us just the way we are. We are accepted because he is the Accepter. We need to remind ourselves that we are beautiful people even though our bodies carry around excess weight.

My friend Ruth, at that time forty pounds over-weight, said to me, "Do you know who I am? I'm a svelte, one-hundred-ten-pound woman with lots of charm who's living in a one-hundred-fifty-pound body."

Ruth was on the right track. She saw herself as beautiful, as acceptable, and she was.

God, help me to realize that though I may sometimes think of myself as an ugly duckling, I'm a beautiful swan waiting to break out. I am acceptable to you regardless of how much I weigh. Amen.

LOVABLE ME

This is my commandment: Love each other in the same way I have loved you. (John 15:12)

Week 4, Day 2

In the past five years I've learned to like myself very much. I believe exercise and a sensible diet have played a large role in this. Whenever I look at myself in the mirror, I'm not ashamed of my physique. I like what I see.

It wasn't always that way. For a long time before losing weight I thought I had things wrong with me. If I couldn't control my appetite, I reasoned, then I was inordinate (a good biblical word), and that made me guilty, which only reinforced my idea of something being wrong with me.

For many of us, we go on a diet to deprive ourselves of good food because we're bad, or we don't measure up to our standards, or we're trying hard to be good, or we want to please our mates or our parents.

What we often fail to understand is that we're okay now—just the way we are. We are acceptable—even if we're one hundred pounds overloaded on the scale and five sizes of clothes too big.

Being a size 5 doesn't make a person more acceptable to God. Losing the fifty unsightly pounds doesn't make one loved.

I remember a girl in high school who had always been overweight and we called her "jelly belly." When she reached her teens, one summer she shed those pounds. When she returned to school in the fall, all the guys noticed her and she had more dates than she could keep tack of.

"Jelly belly" didn't realize that beneath those rolls of fat lived a warm, sensitive, and beautiful girl. Unfortunately, I didn't realize it either, and I was as guilty as the rest in calling her names.

I saw her a few years ago on one of my home-town visits. Still the trim lady, she's now happily married, with children. I confessed to her how badly I felt about the way I had treated her.

"I let you get away with it," she said, "Because I believed you. You can't fight truth." She also said that she was in her mid-twenties before she met the man who became her husband. She had started putting weight on again and while he encouraged her to stay trim, he also told her, "I love you in anything from a size 3 to 53." And he meant it. She was loved for herself, not her weight or size.

It helped my old school friend to know she was loved. And it should come as no surprise to any Christian that we are loved. Jesus has been telling us that for a long, long time.

Dear Jesus, I am loved. I forget so easily, so keep reminding me. As I count my calories, help me to know that you love me, no matter how large or small I am. Amen.

WANTING TO DIE

Then he went on alone into the wilderness, traveling all day. He sat down under a solitary broom tree and prayed that he might die. "I have had enough, LORD," he said. "Take my life, for I am no better than my ancestors who have already died." (1 Kings 19:4)

Week 4, Day 3

A former fatty said it: "I hated myself so much I wanted to die every day." She also said, after losing over one hundred pounds, "Obesity is a slow form of suicide."

She told me her sad story. She could not stop eating, and day after day the pounds piled up. One time she baked a birthday cake for her son, and before she knew it she had eaten the whole cake herself. In horror and self-disgust, she had to bake another one.

For many in our culture the two words *fat* and *ugly* hold hands because they're considered the same. The fatter we become, the more we hate ourselves. And the more ugly our bodies become, the more we eat to soothe our frustrations, and that starts the cycle all over again. From time to time we inwardly scream, "I hate myself and the whole world hates me and I just want to die."

Elijah wanted to die, too. If not literally, at least he was that depressed. His reasons did not stem from the same cause, but he looked upon himself as a failure and a spiritual washout. All he could do finally was to say, "Lord, it would be better for the whole world if you'd just kill me."

God didn't take Elijah's life, and he doesn't want to take our lives away from us, either. Our loving God wants to preserve us. And part of the preserving is to remind us that we're loved by him.

It took me a long, long time to believe I was loved. I thought I wasn't good enough to be loved. I had failed a million times. The reasons went on and on. I had to break that cycle of thinking.

But because of the Bible's central message, encapsulated in John 3:16 ("For God so loved the world that he gave…") I could believe I was loved.

For nearly six months, every morning when I brushed my teeth I looked myself in the face (even with all my flabby pounds still bouncing around my middle) and said, "Cec, you are loved because God made you lovable." Every day I repeated those or similar words. It took six months before I believed it. I had told myself for years that I was a failure, ugly, and stupid. Because I had said those negative words so many times, I had learned to believe them. I had to say it the other way: "Cec, you're beautiful, bright, and gifted."

I learned to believe it. You can, too.

Lord God, I am loved and I am beautiful because I am yours. Just belonging to you makes me lovable. Help me remember that today. Amen.

Afraid to Be Thin

But when I am afraid, I will put my trust in you. (Psalm 56:3)

Week 4, Day 4

Some people find advantages in extra weight. For one thing, they don't have to compete in sports or physical activities. They get to say things like, "My hips, you know…" One fat lady said, "If I lost weight, other men would find me attractive and I'd probably leave my husband." She figured out that as long as she remained fat (that is, ugly), other men would not make passes at her. That kept her marriage safe.

Sometimes fat people get fatter to hide their anger. If they didn't drown themselves in mashed potatoes and extra helpings of chocolate mousse, they'd yell and scream. So they eat more and suppress their anger.

Staying fat provides a wonderful cover for avoiding self-discovery. It's almost as if tissues of fat keep people from looking inward and facing themselves. When we're overweight, we don't have to worry about others' approval, either (we know we don't have it anyway). We never quite find out who we are inside, what our potential is, or what our special gifts are. We're too busy covering up—literally and figuratively!

Not that we fat folks are the only ones who avoid reality. Others just choose other ways of coping. Dave, for instance, always has a wisecrack handy. When you try to get serious with him, he imitates famous comedians to change the tone of things. He doesn't want to be a fallible human, because to be human is to be vulnerable, and to be vulnerable means to be stripped down to the bare soul. Those of us who are (or were) overweight know how frightening that can be.

David knew what it was like to be afraid. He ran from King Saul, who wanted to kill him. He dwelt in the country of the Philistines, sworn enemies of the Jews. He lived in constant peril. But in Psalm 56:3 he says, "When I am afraid, I put my trust in thee." He continues in the psalm to say that no matter what people do to him, he trusts in God's goodness without fear.

All-knowing God, enable me to face myself and not to be afraid to be thin. Enable me to trust you more and know that you want only good for me. Amen.

FORGIVE ME AS I FORGIVE ME

… Be kind to each other, tenderhearted, forgiving one another, just as God through Christ has forgiven you. (Ephesians 4:32)

Week 4, Day 5

Fat people don't forgive themselves easily. That's one grand reason they keep the extra poundage. They go on a diet and after losing the first four pounds, stumble and fall for a thick milk shake or a juicy fried steak. Then they pile on the misery and self-condemnation. I know. I've been there.

We not only can't forgive ourselves, but we compensate by pointing out everyone else's shortcomings. We get beyond tearing down others when we can accept our own failures and forgive ourselves.

We need to remind ourselves that we're human. We all fail at times. We can acknowledge it and forgive ourselves.

I found the Lord's Prayer helpful when I was in the early stages of my calorie counting. "Forgive us our debts/trespasses…." I had not intended to fail, but being human I did. I fail in hundreds of other ways, too. But no matter what kind of failure—from overindulgence to disobedience of a major commandment—God still forgives. And because he forgives me, I can forgive me, too.

Forgiving God, forgive me when I fail and help me forgive me, also. Amen.

FAT DEPRESSION

Think about the things of heaven, not the things of earth.
(Colossians 3:2)

Week 4, Day 6

I lost twenty-five pounds. I had reached my goal. Most of the time I felt good about myself. I would look in the mirror in the bathroom with satisfaction. When walking down the street I would glance at my reflection in the store windows. It felt good to have a trim stomach and not to feel the pressure of my clothes pulling at the seams.

But even after I had lost my weight, I went through what I call the fat depression. I looked at myself in the mirror and knew I was thinner. I knew that my waistline had trimmed four inches, but somehow I still tended to think of myself as chubby.

I talked to other former fatties about this. Sometimes they lose the weight in their bodies before they lose it in their heads. The fatter we are, the poorer our self-image. Sometimes we lose the weight from our bodies, but the mental change takes longer.

Upon realizing this, I printed a little sign which I kept on my typewriter at the office and on my dresser at home: *Think thin.* I began to consider myself a thin person rather than an overstuffed one. It took a while for my behavior and mental attitude to catch up with the new body I was wearing.

The same thing happened to me after my conversion. I was a Christian. I tried to follow the Lord. But sometimes I reverted back to former behavior or at least thought in ways I knew didn't please God. Occasionally I had spells of depression and would say to myself, "If I'm really a Christian, why do I think like that?" Part of the reason again is that it takes time for all these things to change. Perhaps I expected an overnight transformation that would change my behavior, my mental attitude, and my affections.

The Apostle Paul might have had something like that in mind when he wrote to the Colossians. He said that they had been raised with Christ, and they ought to seek those things that pertained to Christ. "Set your minds on things that are above, not on things that are on earth."

As a Christian, I sometimes need to make a mental sign for myself: THINK HEAVENWARD.

Lord Jesus, I am still a new person, a thinner person. Help me to get over these fat depressions and to think thin. Amen.

HANDLING ANGER

And "don't sin by letting anger control you." Don't let the sun go down while you are still angry. (Ephesians 4:26)

Week 4, Day 7

Everybody likes Opal. She's sweet and even-tempered. No one ever has heard her speak a cross word. When difficulties strike or problems seem to turn her family upside down, Opal takes everything calmly. She's also nearly a hundred pounds overweight.

Without being simplistic about it, I'm convinced that one of the causes of Opal's weight problem is the fact that she cannot acknowledge her anger. One time she and I talked about anger, and she said, "Good Christians never lose their tempers."

I didn't say this, but I thought, "So they eat instead." We sometimes get the idea that we cannot be good Christians if we get angry. Paul says, "Be angry, but don't sin in doing it." There are times when all of us get angry about things. The issue is not so much the anger, but how we channel our anger. When we handle it in destructive ways, it becomes sin.

Jesus cleansed the temple because peddlers had desecrated it. Jesus used a whip and chased them out. He said, "You've made my Father's house a den of thieves." That was anger—good anger.

Anger is a very human emotion. It's all right to be angry, but we often need help in how to use and channel it. Fat folks tend to stuff their mouths and stomachs with food rather than cope with their emotions.

Here are a few things that I have found helpful in handling my own anger.

Express it. Say to the person, "I am angry with you." Let the individual know that you are not happy. That's a good way of getting it straightened out.

Talk to a supportive person. Sometimes you can't tell the person that you're angry at, but you can tell someone else to help you and support you in dealing with your anger.

Divert it into other activities. Sometimes we're angry over an injustice or a slight and there's nothing we can do about it. Exercise is one good way of diverting anger.

When I'm angry, I find that running does wonders for me. I start to run with stomach muscles tense from ill feelings. By the time I have completed running, all that anger has disappeared. I have acknowledged my anger and chosen not to use it destructively.

Almighty God, help me to acknowledge my anger and to use it creatively, but never as a means of sinning. Amen.

Exercise Profits

Physical training is good, but training for godliness is much better, promising benefits in this life and in the life to come. (1 Timothy 4:8)

Week 5, Day 1

We have learned that diet accompanied by a strenuous exercise is far more effective than diet alone—especially for those who stay with an exercise program.

Not only do we lose weight when we exercise and diet, but this reduces the rate of heart attacks, high blood pressure, and a lot of other kinds of illnesses. We know exercise can help prevent strokes. There's also good evidence to indicate that we need to burn up at least two thousand calories a week in physical activities as a good preventative against heart attack. We know that exercise and a good diet plan enables people to be more cheerful and emotionally stable. Exercise enables us to lessen stress.

Paul wrote to Timothy that physical exercise profits a little bit. He was saying that there is value in physical exercise. The rest of the verse tells us that even better than exercise is godliness, valuable in every way. We don't want to deny the importance of physical exercise, but many times people are too physically worn out and too tired to keep their spiritual life up. We want to be godly people, and part of the way we achieve godliness is through counting our calories, enriched by a good but moderate exercise program which gives us the energy to spend time in prayer and Bible reading.

Dear Lord, as I count my calories and exercise my body, help me remember that as important as these are, it's even more important to exercise godliness in all my life. Amen.

MIRACLE BODY

Thank you for making me so wonderfully complex! Your workmanship is marvelous—how well I know it. (Psalm 139:14)

Week 5, Day 2

We often fail to realize that our bodies are miracles in themselves. They have marvelous recuperative powers and heal themselves in ways we still can't figure out.

What amazes me as much as anything is the way the human diet works. In a wise and wonderful way, God has constituted the body so that it changes food into the essential bodily needs. For instance, among cultures where animal flesh is uneaten, good nourishment takes place through what we call complementary proteins, such as beans and brown rice eaten together. In other cultures, where they ingest almost nothing but meat, the body can manufacture glucose from proteins and fats.

What many don't realize is the importance of the three major fuels of metabolism—the products which give us energy and health for our bodies.

Proteins. The principal function of protein is to provide building blocks for vital organs, muscular tissue, and body chemicals. When protein is eaten in amounts beyond these needs, it converts into carbohydrate or fat. Proteins are aggregations of amino acids, some of which the body can self-manufacture (often called nonessential amino acids) and others which can come only from food (essential amino acids). Any good diet *must* contain these proteins.

Fats. These storage fats (triglycerides) provide two major metabolic fuels, free fatty acids and ketone bodies. When stored fat breaks down to provide energy, these fuels are freed. Some fats must be provided by the food we eat, and are called essential fatty acids because the body cannot manufacture them.

Proteins and fats occur together in animal products such as meat, fish, fowl, eggs, and cheese.

Carbohydrates. Carbohydrates come mainly from vegetables. They provide a large share of the metabolic fuel in our westernized diets and break down into glucose, the major fuel of metabolism.

What does all this say? That this body, this holy temple, devised and created by God, is a miracle in itself.

Creator God, I am a miracle. Help me care for this miracle by the food I put into it, and teach me to feed it only that which truly nourishes it. Amen.

ENERGY LEVEL

In your strength I can crush an army; with my God I can scale any wall. (Psalm 18:29)

Week 5, Day 3

Even though Eleanor's weight hovered in the average range, she had a listless feeling most of the time and had to push herself to accomplish normal tasks.

Betty started out her day with normal energy. By midmorning, weakness overtook her and by noon she felt dizzy spells and her hands shook.

Both women discovered that they had dietary deficiencies. Eleanor simply was anemic, and once her doctor had built up her hemoglobin she made certain that her diet contained iron-rich items such as grape juice and blackstrap molasses.

Betty suffered from hypoglycemia (low blood sugar), and by eliminating all sugar and eating a high-protein diet, she has successfully overcome the symptoms.

Both women discovered two things: (1) the amount of consumed food alone provides no full answer; (2) wrong foods or lack of proper ones can cause harm.

We're discovering more fully all the time that what we eat affects not only our weight, but our behavior. Recently a hyperactive five-year-old boy, after a strict change of diet, eliminating foods containing sugar and certain food dyes, changed into a child of normal energy.

As we count our calories and shed the pounds, we want a diet that gives us the energy to maintain our daily routines.

The psalmist speaks of leaping over a wall. What a picture of energy! On our calorie counting programs we may not always feel like leaping over walls, but if we're faithful and select a sensible diet, we'll have the energy to do what needs to be done.

A sensible, well-balanced diet, followed faithfully, provides sufficient needed energy—if not enough to leap over a wall, at least enough to run a mile.

Lord God, give me the energy I need for today as I count my calories in my service to you. Amen.

A GOOD FIGHT

I have fought the good fight, I have finished the race, and I have remained faithful. (2 Timothy 4:7)

Week 5, Day 4

When I made my decision to lose weight, I realized it was going to be a battle. I had tried various times before to lose weight and had given up after a couple of weeks. This time I was serious. I had learned as much as I possibly could about losing weight; now I was going to fight, and I was going to win.

I made an important decision: ice cream would disappear from my diet. I had no intentions of going on a crash diet, getting to a specified weight, and start eating any way I chose. I determined to fight the weight problem the rest of my life.

I also made some other decisions. I would learn to like raw vegetables and fruit. I seldom ate either.

No one ever said it would be easy to lose weight. Most of us accumulate a pound or two here and there in our early twenties to mid-twenties. Only when we awaken to the fact that we are grossly over-weight and need to do something about it do we put up a fight.

And it is a fight. Temptations come our way through the food we constantly see advertised on television. We go to dinners or banquets and some-one always urges us to eat the fattening foods. With little smiles they say, "Oh, this one time won't hurt." Part of what we have to do is learn to smile in return and say, "No, thank you." When we do that often enough, we know we have won and we can keep on winning.

For most of us the battle against increasing weight will be a lifetime struggle. We need to make our minds up to that. But knowing it's a battle ena-bles us to keep our defenses up and to stay on the lookout for our enemy—our appetite.

The Apostle Paul viewed the Christian life in the same way. In the last letter he wrote, he said that he had fought the good fight, he'd kept the faith. He went on to say that there was a crown laid up for him because he had done his best and he had won. I don't know about crowns for losing weight. I do know this, that I had to get rid of all my clothes when I slimmed down. I can't think of a better trophy in the battle of weight loss than a new wardrobe.

Holy Spirit, help me in my battle against calories, so that I can be a slimmer me. Amen.

WINNING THE RACE

All athletes are disciplined in their training. They do it to win a prize that will fade away, but we do it for an eternal prize. (1 Corinthians 9:25)

Week 5, Day 5

Shortly after Shirley and I married, I realized that she was usually still eating her meal after I had completely finished. No one had ever called my attention to the fact that I wolfed down my food. I remember my pattern of gulping down the food, feeling absolutely stuffed, and then an hour later wondering why I was so hungry.

Years lapsed before I tried to do anything about that. I realized that I ate too fast, but did not know what to do about it. One day I had an idea. Why not race with other people? But this race would be different. Instead of my racing to finish first, I would aim to be the last one done. One rule I imposed: None of my eating companions would know about the game.

I discovered several ways to help me slow down. For one thing, I began to chew my food more thoroughly. That was hard for me, because I normally took about three bites and swallowed. Now I consciously chewed my food. I also made it a point that after every two or three mouthfuls of food, I stopped to take a sip of water. When I took that sip I'd put my knife and fork down. I even wiped my lips with a napkin.

As another method, I tried to talk a good deal during the meal. I also began paying more attention to the texture of the food and to think about how it tasted. Sometimes I even paused over each item and just smelled it.

I learned that I could win the game, and frequently did. By the end of meal time, I felt full. There's a time lag for the signals traveling from the stomach to the brain notifying it that food has arrived. When we eat too fast, the hunger won't be satisfied in the brain until long after the stomach has received more than enough. In slowing down I actually learned to eat less and to enjoy my food more.

Every time I won the meal competition, I thought of these words from the Apostle Paul. In 1 Corinthians 9:24-26, he compares the Christian life to running a race. He emphasizes the importance of discipline and self-control in order to win. In many ways, being a calorie counter is like running a race, but my race goes backwards. I'm trying to lengthen the time I eat, slow down the amount I eat, and increase my appreciation for the quality of the food while the quantity decreases.

This has now become such a common part of my eating experience that I no longer consciously play the game of trying to be the last one done. However, I am still usually the last one to finish. Each time I'm aware that I'm the last one finished I chuckle a bit and think to myself, *Well, Cec, the Lord has helped you win another race.*

Lord God, teach me self-control as I count my calories, so that I can offer you a better body for your service. Amen.

Running: The Miracle Answer

All athletes are disciplined in their training. They do it to win a prize that will fade away, but we do it for an eternal prize. So I run with purpose in every step. I am not just shadowboxing. (1 Corinthians 9:25–26)

Week 5, Day 6

Oh-oh, you've heard that before about running. But it works, and I speak from experience. Once I got into running, the weight melted off my body.

In order for jogging to offer the maximum benefit, along with calorie counting, we need to exercise at least thirty minutes three times a week. (If you're in good shape, you can drop that down to twice weekly.) Think of the advantages of running.

No competition. One of the problems we overweight types struggle with is judging ourselves by comparing ourselves with others. We can jog all alone. We have no standards to meet.

We decide how far and how long to run. In the beginning I spent half of my time walking. That's okay, too, but running is better because our bodies burn up calories faster.

We can jog almost anywhere and at any time of day. I jog three times a week, sometimes four. I don't always do it the same hour and vary my place of running to ward off boredom, but I do run.

Jogging improves the self-image. The more I run, the better I feel about myself. Anger dissipates and tension leaves. Although often tired, I finish a running day with a good inner feeling.

Jogging improves overall physical condition, and not only weight loss. I found added benefits such as a lowered blood pressure and a stronger heart.

Jogging rewards early. Within a month I found my clothes hanging looser and my waistline slimming. Even better, other people noticed, too.

It is spiritually valuable. I not only lost weight through jogging, but I often meditate and come home feeling more alert. It's also an answer to chronic depression.

In the past two years I have paid little attention to the amount of food I eat. My activity level with jogging regulates that for me. I still weigh myself every day, and I vary as much as two pounds within a week, but I now weigh less than I did at age twenty-two. The Lord has used jogging to make me a winner at the losing game. I believe I'm a better disciple of Jesus Christ today because of my jogging.

Lord, help me get into physical activity and stay with it. I ask this not only for the physical benefit and the weight loss, but because of all of the other benefits as well. Amen.

Doing It Together

Two people are better off than one, for they can help each other succeed. If one person falls, the other can reach out and help. But someone who falls alone is in real trouble. (Ecclesiastes 4:9–10)

Week 5, Day 7

When I started calorie counting, I had an extra bonus: Shirley joined me. We worked together. We had meals in our home that aided our weight-loss program.

It was more than cooperation in the food department. We talked about weight. I mentioned how I felt about carrying a football pouch around my waist. One morning I tried to run across the parking lot of the church and found myself winded halfway there. I told Shirley how it embarrassed me to hear people call me chubby or chunky.

We relied on and encouraged each other. I remember one day I bought a new suit. I went from a bursting-at-the-seams size 40 to a trim 38 that hung loose. I liked what I saw in the mirror. Even more, I'll never forget the sparkle in Shirley's eyes. "You haven't looked that good since we first married," she said.

We understood each other. We sympathized when the other fell in moments of temptation. We also goaded and scolded if necessary.

In other areas I've discovered the value of having a partner. Last year Dave and I, as members of a sharing group, both realized that our devotional reading hit ups and downs. I'd skip a day, sometimes as many as three, and then feel guilty and goad myself onward again. The same things happened to Dave. We agreed to pray for each other daily. Further, each morning I called Dave (or he called me, whatever we arranged), and we helped each other get into the routine of daily praying and Bible reading.

We learned by experience the words of the preacher in Ecclesiastes who tells us that two are better than one.

If you don't have a partner and don't belong to Overeaters Anonymous, TOPS (Take Off Pounds Sensibly), or a similar group, don't count calories alone. Find an overweight buddy who wants to take it off, too. Select a person you can feel close to and who's not judgmental when you fail. You also don't want an overindulgent type who says, "Poor friend, that's all right."

A partner gives encouragement when you need it. When I got stuck at seven pounds above my goal, I could not seem to get beyond. Every day I counted calories and stuck to it. But that scale persisted in giving me the same answer for over a week. "Just keep it up," Shirley would say. She didn't understand *why*, but she kept consoling me.

One morning I got on the scale and to my delight saw the indicator drop a whole four pounds. Shirley had shared my frustration. Now she could share my joy.

Father, give me a loving partner in my calorie counting, so that we can encourage each other. Amen.

If you already have a partner, try this one:

Father, thank you for my partner. May we constantly encourage each other as we aim for slimmer bodies and better health. Amen.

WATCH IT!

Stay alert! Watch out for your great enemy, the devil. He prowls around like a roaring lion, looking for someone to devour. Stand firm against him, and be strong in your faith. Remember that your Christian brothers and sisters all over the world are going through the same kind of suffering you are. (1 Peter 5:8, 9)

Week 6, Day 1

We had already started eliminating sweets in our home, but occasionally Shirley would bake cookies for our son. One day she made pea-nut-butter cookies. I stood in the kitchen talking to her and without consciously thinking, I picked up a cookie, ate it, and reached for a second before it hit me: I don't eat cookies.

This illustrates what happens to us if we're not vigilant and careful. We think that because we make up our minds to go on a diet we'll be all right. Sometimes we forget, or we put ourselves in situations where we cannot resist the urge. The next thing we know, we've given in. I have a friend who does very well with dieting except that she's constantly accepting invitations to have tea or brunch at someone's home. She knows that they will have a lot of rich desserts that she ought not to eat. She always goes with the idea, "Oh, I can handle it." She always gives in and says to herself afterward, *I won't do that again.* But she always does.

Peter exhorts us to be watchful. He compares the devil to a roaring lion seeking to devour any and all of us. Our appetites are just as much like a lion. They've been trained to consume anything that we put into our bodies, and to make us hunger for things that we don't need. It's important for us to learn to watch out not only in our eating, but in all areas of our lives.

Lord Jesus, keep me watchful so that I won't give in when temptation comes my way. Amen.

How to Win

Stay alert! Watch out for your great enemy, the devil. He prowls around like a roaring lion, looking for someone to devour. (1 Peter 5:8)

Week 6, Day 2

We have to try all kinds of ways to win in the calorie-counting game. We have gained our weight over the years by carelessness and indifference. Now we have to wage all-out warfare.

In our warfare, we have different tactics. One I capitalize on is my desire to have people's approval of my actions. I can gain approval, or at least respect, by stating my position and holding onto it. If I say I do not eat desserts, no matter how much my stomach says I want them, I cannot give in; I won't let myself.

Peter warns us that the devil is like a roaring lion. Sometimes that devil attacks us in the forms of our appetites and our old habits. Peter says that the best way to fight is to stay alert and to watch out.

One trick I learned: At most formal dinners I discovered that they serve the salad on large lettuce leaves which most people don't eat. I spend a great deal of time carefully and slowly eating those lettuce leaves and pass up the congealed salad, which is usually sugar laden. We all learn little tricks if we want to win the game.

It's like guerrilla warfare. We try anything that works and defeats our fatty lumps. We learn little tricks that enable us to overcome our appetites and bad eating habits. We want to train our appetites to not be roaring lions but to be submissive; otherwise the devil defeats us. Because of Christ in our lives, we know we can win.

Lord Jesus, you are more powerful than my appetite and all the other forces in the world. Help me to overcome temptation and to become victorious in my calorie counting. Amen.

BACKSLIDING

Bring Mark with you when you come, for he will be helpful to me in my ministry. (2 Timothy 4:11)

Week 6, Day 3

I have a favorite story in the New Testament. It concerns a young man, John Mark. He's mentioned in Acts and in one of Paul's letters. When Paul and Barnabas (John Mark's uncle) went on their first missionary trip, they took John Mark along. Perhaps because of the difficulties of travel, the constant persecution, or the many deprivations, he went home. Later Barnabas and Paul split over John Mark. Paul refused to take a quitter with him on a second trip. Barnabas took Mark anyway.

You read no more about this young man in the Book of Acts. And if that had been the whole story it would have been a tragedy. In Paul's last letter, the second one to Timothy, he writes this strange sentence: "Get Mark and bring him with you; for he is very useful in serving me." The first time I read that statement, I could hardly believe it. Here was a man who had turned his back on God and on God's service and had failed. Yet the last word we have of him is not denunciation and judgment. Instead, he receives a badge of commendation. Paul says, "He's useful in serving me."

Tradition tells us that John Mark was the scribe who wrote the Gospel bearing his name. Probably Peter dictated it and Mark did the actual writing. Another badge of commendation.

I share this story because most of us calorie counters go through periods of backsliding. We don't intend to, but we do. We plan to get on our diet, stay with it, and not stop until we're a beautifully thin, attractive person. But sometimes we fail.

We fail, if not in our diet, in our human relationships by loving too little or not forgiving enough. If that were the end of our story, it would be a tragedy.

The real story for us is that God forgives (1 John 1:9). When we confess our failure and ask God to strengthen us, then we can get back on our calorie counting again.

Lord Jesus, forgive my failures as a Christian and as a calorie counter. Amen.

Getting Off
to a Fat Start

Even if my father and mother abandon me, the Lord will hold me close. (Psalm 27:10)

Week 6, Day 4

A lot of overweight folks started life that way. In fact, when our own children were small, people kept trying to fatten them up. "Why, that baby hardly eats at all." The picture of blubbery cheeks and fat bodies implies health. It also implies a fat start in life.

This is not a put-the-blame-on-Mom-and-Dad jag, but think about your childhood. Parents and older folks often used food for the wrong purpose. "You be quiet in church and you can have an ice-cream cone on the way home." Ever get a candy bar for cleaning up your room or taking out the garbage? How about a hot fudge sundae for being extra nice to grandparents? Remember the time you brought home a bad paper from school and you cried about it? What did Mom do? Stuffed you with cookies, hugged you, and said, "It's okay, darling."

Some kids start toward fatness because insecure parents can't say no. The noisy brat demands a candy bar, and Dad feels the boy won't love him if he says no. Because their friends fill up on potato chips, fast-food burgers, and pizzas, loving parents give in or else the children might question how much they're loved.

I have one distinct memory of a time when I left home angry. I was twelve or thirteen years old. It was one of those nobody-loves-me days and I was too big to cry. I remember also that I had four dollars I had earned from carrying newspapers. I went to a soda fountain and drank two full malted milks and ate a handful of Hershey bars. Later I bought peanuts and another malted milk. I was also sick that night. But during the day, I forgot my pain of feeling unloved.

All kinds of things happen to us in our childhood that give us a push toward obesity. It won't help to blame Mom and Dad. They did the best they knew how.

We can remind ourselves that Mom and Dad probably failed in 173 ways in life—in the same way that those of us who are parents fail our children. But there's one who never fails. His name is Jesus. He sets the example for us and says, "You can do it. You can lose weight and I'll help you."

When you're struggling most with your fat-prone body, ask his help. He's eager to help you count the calories and trim off the excess.

All-seeing Lord, thank you that you never fail me. Help me remain faithful to you as I work at losing my excess weight. Amen.

COMPULSION

They are headed for destruction. Their god is their appetite,
they brag about shameful things, and they think only about
this life here on earth. (Philippians 3:19)

Week 6, Day 5

Compulsive eaters are laden with guilt. And
many of them can figure out no way to win.
They often view eating foods such as ice cream and
pie as felonies or illegal, other foods such as bananas
as misdemeanors. They consider foods such as fish
and chicken (not fried, please) as legal. The whole
system tends to add to the guilt syndrome. They
have only a few legal foods left.

The system gets tough for the compulsive eaters.
They fail by eating one potato chip (and, as the com-
mercial goes, they can't stop with just one). They eat
and not only continue to eat, but actually eat faster.

Compulsive eaters withdraw from food as a way
of being good. But they can abstain only so long, and
when they start eating again, they have no control.
Food acts as drug, and they eat and force it down.
It's as though the food must be eaten quickly so that

it is no longer dangerous. Once consumed, the crisis has passed. All the compulsive eater has left is the memory of a food binge, hundreds of extra calories ingested, and a heavy load of guilt.

Compulsive eaters end up with the words of the Apostle Paul ringing in their ears: "...their god is the belly...." They have bowed at the shrine and now have given homage to their demanding god.

The good news to Christians is that our bellies are not our gods. We need not feel guilty over our binges. When we overindulge, we confess and pray, "Give me strength to resist next time." And because we confess, we have the assurance of Jesus' words, "Go, and do not sin again." We are free—free not to overindulge, free to overcome our compulsion. And we can!

Master of Life, I'm one of those compulsive eaters. I need help and I need forgiveness. Give me both, as I know you will. Amen.

Responsibility

Everything is pure to those whose hearts are pure. But nothing is pure to those who are corrupt and unbelieving, because their minds and consciences are corrupted. (Titus 1:15)

Week 6, Day 6

"Oh, those terrible banana splits," she said as she passed the Baskin-Robbins store. "If I could just get that stuff out of my sight, I could really lose weight."

Not true, friend. I didn't say that, of course. But she blamed food for her problem. That's a common fallacy.

The real problem lives inside the head. It's attitudinal. The successful calorie counters know this. They don't write out long lists of "bad" foods and "good" foods.

When I was twenty-five pounds overweight, I concentrated on what I ate and how much. I got the upper hand when I began to think of food as neutral. It was my attitude which made the difference in the amount I ate and the choices I made.

Once I accepted that fact, I admitted that I am responsible for myself and my actions. I had to do more than lose weight. I also had to want to lose it and to keep it off. The blame for extra pounds doesn't rest on the dietician, the family, or my doctor. It's my responsibility.

When I sit down at a table now and survey a wide variety of food, none of it is bad. Some foods offer less nutrition, a few may not be personally to my liking, but the food is neutral. I have the power to say no to anything on the table.

When I slip (and I do occasionally), I can no longer blame a friend for putting all those tempting foods in front of me. I can't blame the waiter for loading down my plate with more food than my body needs. Problems, chaos, or wars cannot be scapegoats. When I fail, I take the blame. When I overcome, I accept the credit.

I also pray about my weight. As a Christian, I want everything in my life to honor Jesus Christ. I want to be a living example of the Christian faith. The corpulent, greedy, and guilt-laden individual doesn't do much to advance the cause of the Lord.

By accepting responsibility for all my actions and behavior, I learn how to cope. I learn to say, "Help me, Lord, because I am weak." But I don't blame a scapegoat.

Lord Jesus, thank you for all the food in the world you've made for us to eat. Help me take responsibility for my eating habits today. Amen.

CELEBRATING

Thank God! He gives us victory over sin and death through our Lord Jesus Christ. (1 Corinthians 15:57)

Week 6, Day 7

The big day came for me. I had reached my goal of twenty-five pounds lost and the scales verified it. I had achieved my goal. A celebration of some type seemed in order.

I bought myself a new pair of slacks. After all, I had lost nearly four inches in the midsection, and my pants had all been taken in or hung on me as though they belonged to an older and bigger brother. It gave me a great lift to go into the men's department, try on a pair of slacks, and view myself in the mirror. I felt trim and fit that day.

And why not celebrate? That's part of our way of life. Every time we accomplish a goal, win an award, or overcome an obstacle, our culture says, "Now we celebrate."

I have one friend who has trouble with celebrating. He aims for 190 pounds and as soon as he achieves his goal, after weeks of near-starving, he goes out for a huge meal. The next morning he gets angry because he gains as much as two or three pounds *overnight.*

We need the joy of celebrating—healthy celebration. Indulging in rich desserts or second helpings or everything in sight only sets us up for the yo-yo syndrome, and we're back struggling with the pounds again.

Instead, let's try creative ways of celebrating. Buy yourself something to wear as I suggested. Or a bottle of bath lotion. One woman dashed over to the beauty shop and came away with a new perm and a lighter hair color.

Celebrating for calorie counters reinforces *to ourselves* that we're making it. We've done something significant. Losing even ten pounds means that we've had the willpower to stick with our commitment. We need to appreciate our victories.

We also need to take time to say thanks to God. I prayed a lot during my battle with my bulge. (I still pray for God to make me temperate in my eating habits.) I'm the slimmer me because of his help and, like the Apostle Paul, I like to pause from time to time to say, "Thanks, God, for the overwhelming victory we have through Jesus Christ."

Victorious Jesus, thank you for victory over each pound of fat that I dump. Keep me celebrating in healthy ways. Amen.

Self-Help Reminders
for Dieters

1. No fad diet or pill can alter overweight eating habits. Only *I* can change them.
2. I am setting an eating style *for the rest of my life.* I am not going to quit when I reach my desired weight. I'll always be conscious of what I eat.
3. The faster I lose weight, the more likely I am to regain it unless I alter my long-term eating habits. Weight control requires effort and a change of life-style.
4. Most overweight people eat too fast. There is a lag between the time food enters the mouth and travels to the stomach and the signal reaches the brain. Quick eating won't satisfy me until after my stomach has received more food than I need. I will consciously learn to slow down my eating time.
5. Some foods help me slow up my eating such as cauliflower, lettuce, celery, cucumbers, broccoli, and cabbage. They also have negligible calories, and I can eat them in almost unlimited amounts.

6. Bay windows are out of style. I will work toward trim lines.

7. The best exercise: pushing myself away from the table. The next best: running, because it's inexpensive, can be done almost anywhere at any season, and provides one of the best, all-around exercise programs.

8. In addition to a sensible diet, I can help my weight-loss program by daily exercise. If I expend more energy than I take in through food, I lose weight. Many people feel they have less appetite and actually consume less food after exercising.

9. If I take in only one hundred extra calories every day, I will gain ten pounds in one year. If I eat one hundred calories less every day than I need, I can lose ten pounds a year.

10. I will not eat only one meal a day. It's more fattening. When I eat a large meal, my body secretes more digestive juices and I actually digest the food faster. Consequently, I become hungry soon after a meal. It's easier and healthier to digest smaller meals. My body also needs nourishment more than once a day. I can divide up my total calories for the day into six meals instead of three.

11. Negative emotions cause me to overeat. When I become aware of anger, anxiety, sadness, or loneliness, I will find corrective ways of dealing with that emotion rather than by eating.

12. As I achieve goals in my weight-loss pro-
     gram, I will celebrate through buying or
     doing something nice for myself (but not by
     eating).

13. I will remind myself regularly that I am beau-
     tiful, acceptable, and lovable to God, no mat-
     ter what my weight.

14. I will remind myself that this body I live in is
     also God's house.

15. I want to lose weight. I will be less prone to
     diseases such as diabetes, heart conditions,
     and high blood pressure.

16. Because God wants me at my best, he will
     help me in my calorie counting.

More Self-Help Reminders for Dieters

1. I will focus on my lifestyle. I choose to eat carefully, not only to lose weight but because I will choose to eat this way for the rest of my life.
2. I want my spiritual commitment to show not only in the way I talk, live, and treat others but also by the way I take care for my body.
3. I will not condemn myself when I fail. Instead I will say, "I forgive myself and I'll do better next time."
4. I will enlist caring friends or relatives to help me remain faithful to my commitment to a thinner body and a healthier lifestyle.
5. I will never say, "I can't eat _____." Instead I will say, "I can eat anything I want, but I choose not to eat certain things."

EXCERPT FROM

DEVOTIONS FOR RUNNERS

WEIGHTED RUNNING

Therefore, since we are surrounded by such a huge crowd of witnesses to the life of faith, let us strip off every weight that slows us down, especially the sin that so easily trips us up. And let us run with endurance the race God has set before us. (Hebrews 12:1)

A Greek myth tells about Atalanta, a huntress nursed from infancy by a bear. As she grew older, she gained fame for her physical prowess, by hunting and running faster than any man. When Atalanta reached marriageable age, she turned down her suitors. "I will only marry the man who can outrun me," she said.

The challengers came. Atalanta defeated and humiliated them all. Her father had all the would-be husbands killed.

One bright fellow named Hippomenes (in some books they call him Milanion) came along. He knew that he could not possibly outrun her. He had to figure out a way to beat her, become her husband, and inherit half of the vast kingdom. After weeks of thought, Hippomenes came up with a sure-fire way to win.

The two started the race, and Hippomenes gave a great burst of speed which he knew he could not maintain. As soon as Atalanta got close to him, he pulled a golden apple out of a bag he carried, dropped it, and moved on. She, knowing she could pass the man easily, stopped, and picked up the golden object.

Minutes later she was ready to pass him again, and Hippomenes dropped another golden apple. She picked it up. The farther they ran, the heavier Atalanta's load became. By the time he had rid himself of his load and she had picked up every apple, he easily won the race, and the hand of Atalanta.

I always think of that mythical race when I read Hebrews 12. The exhortation to "lay aside every weight" makes that story flash into my mind. One runner dropped his burden, the other only accumulated more weight. Over the course of several miles, Hippomenes easily won. He had stripped himself of everything that held him back. Atalanta merely weighted herself down.

We know that in running, the more weight we carry, the harder the race. The fleetest runners wear the lightest shoes and clothes. They're also trim, with almost no body fat. They want nothing impeding them.

As we run the race of life, we're not always so concerned with burdens we carry. Many find themselves loaded down with debts, worries sometimes.

Guilt puts more weight on us than most of us acknowledge.

Perhaps the writer of Hebrews understood this, for he says not only to lay aside weights but also "sin which clings so closely." He exhorts us to have nothing holding us back in our race to follow Jesus Christ. And every weight must ultimately have one name: sin.

No matter what the weight, or how insignificant it may seem, if we allow it to burden us, it impedes our growth and it is sin. These clinging weights come upon us easily.

Even so, we can lay them aside. Through the help of God's Spirit, we can cast aside every weight and "run with perseverance the race that is set before us."

God, I surrender my burdens to you today because you're the world's best weight lifter. Amen.

HITTING THE WALL

But those who trust in the Lord will find new strength. They will soar high on wings like eagles. They will run and not grow weary. They will walk and not faint. (Isaiah 40:31)

Marathoners often talk about "hitting the wall." For most of them, especially the ones new to the grueling demands of 26.2 miles, they know it too well. They run along, depleting their energy and strength, but still moving. Then they awaken to the fact that they can't make it anymore. They've exhausted themselves.

Hitting the wall—the nemesis of runners. We know the experience outside the jogging track as well. You wake up one morning forty-five years old and realize you're in a dead-end job. You're gone as far as you can go. That's the wall.

You've been married for twelve years, and you admit the two of you no longer have a vital, living relationship. You are merely two people who share the same house.

You've tried to teach your children to follow Christ, and now they live in rebellion. You've tried everything to reach them, but their ears become like walls which close you out.

In these and dozens of other situations, what do we do?

We have at least three options: *We can fight.* This attitude says, "I'm gritting my teeth, and I'm going to make it even if I have to crawl. I'm going through that wall."

We stop and give up. We're convinced that the situation is hopeless, and we can't find a solution. We've passed the point of endurance. It's not worth fighting anymore.

We accept it. By accepting, we adjust to life the way it is now. We have no power to change; so we adapt to our new world.

Many hard-rock situations present us with a dilemma. We have no easy answers for many everyday problems. However, we do have the promise in Isaiah 40:31. When we wait upon the Lord (when we pray and wait for his direction), he gives us the answer by renewing our strength. We can then hold out a little longer. We can adapt with grace. We can surrender with strength and peace.

The wall may not be the end at all. Instead it can be an opportunity, an opportunity for us to show God that we need him, an opportunity for God to respond to us. It's a confession of our weakness and our need for his strength. Hitting the wall says,

"Okay, Lord, here's where I need you to take over. I'll never make it without your help."

Then God comes through. We who felt we couldn't make it one more step find ourselves soaring like the eagle.

My teacher and my God, help me learn once and for all that when problems overwhelm me, that's your opportunity to take over and deliver me. Amen.

DEPRESSION

Why am I discouraged? Why is my heart so sad? I will put my hope in God! I will praise him again—my Savior and my God! (Psalm 42:5)

Depression hit me hard. I couldn't throw it off all morning. *Marie's dead,* I kept thinking. She had been so alive the day before, smiling, making plans. She underwent coronary-artery bypass surgery, and the doctor had expected recovery. But because of other medical problems, she died seventeen hours after surgery.

Marie had been active in our church, helping us form a Sunday-school class for divorced singles. She had encouraged and strengthened many when they felt cast down and discouraged.

I dragged through until midafternoon. Things I needed to do no longer seemed important. I couldn't rise above the grief and sense of loss. Finally I went for a five-mile run in the rain. I came back, still sad, but my depression had lifted. I felt normal again.

For me, running has proved valuable in coping with depression. There was a time when I could mope around and ask, as the psalmist did, "Why are you cast down, O my soul?" Now I run.

Something about vigorous activity dulls the impact of negative feelings. Running roots out anger, lessens anxiety, and breaks down hostility.

I see depressed people all the time. They visit my office; they call me on the phone. They're sluggish. They do a minimum of physical movement.

I've often thought that if I had to characterize depressed people by a physical position, I would use words such as *sitting* or *lying down*. That was the position of Elijah when he went through a tough time (1 Kings 19:4) "I have had enough, LORD," he said. "Take my life, for I am no better than my ancestors who have already died" (1 Kings 19:4).

In low times people want to shut themselves away from others. They take the phone off the hook, crawl under the covers, and sleep. Or they sit and stare at nothing for hours. The more they think, the more they brood and fill their minds with morbid thoughts.

Yet when those same people get their marvelously made bodies into action, things change. They may experience physical tiredness, but they also feel better about life and about themselves.

In the years I've been jogging, I've never felt depressed at the end of a workout. I've had aching legs, blistered heels and toes, once or twice even muscle cramps, but never depression. I groan and strain during the run. But when it's all over and I stand under the shower, I find myself singing and enjoying life. I always like myself a lot more and believe God is pleased that I'm trying to take good care of his holy temple.

Thanks, Lord Jesus, for lifting my spirits. With your help, I can overcome all my obstacles. Amen.

About the Author

New York Times bestselling author Cecil (Cec) Murphey has written or co-written more than 135 books, including the bestsellers *90 Minutes in Heaven* (with Don Piper) and *Gifted Hands: The Ben Carson Story* (with Dr. Ben Carson). His books have sold in the millions and have brought hope and encouragement to countless people around the world.

Visit his website at www.CecilMurphey.com and follow him on Twitter at www.Twitter.com/CecMurphey.

www.ingramcontent.com/pod-product-compliance
Lightning Source LLC
Chambersburg PA
CBHW020551030426
42337CB00013B/1055